# 30 DAY BLESSING CHALLENGE

**Releasing God's Goodness over your children.**

Written By:

## ANDRE J. BENJAMIN

COPYRIGHT 2017

Cover design by Jesus Cordero

Book design by Velin@Perseus-Design.com

# LET US KNOW HOW THINGS ARE GOING

## GO TO WWW.CEOOFDESTINY.COM

- Grab FREE GOODIES

- Join the Adventure and Give us updates and we will share best practices, success, challenges and opportunities to see our children live the blessed life.

Daily Blessings for Your Child

# INTRODUCTION

You were designed by God to be a BLESSING MACHINE!

Our children are bombarded with images, ideas, thoughts and information from many sources each moment daily. We have the sacred privilege and honor to release words of life over our children daily that will empower them to prosper even as their soul prospers.

This resources is put together as a challenge for you the parent(s) (and or guardians) for the next 30 days to use as a launching point to bless your children. I encourage you to delve into this book and don't get discouraged or judge by external appearances as to what is happening as you faithfully commit to this process. Seeds when planted are invisible to the human eye. There seemingly is nothing taking place with the seed. There is what lies beneath that matters.

As a child I was given a project at school to plant some seed and see what happens. Well in immense impatience, I continued to dig up the seeds daily and place them back underground. At the end of the period we were to report back, many classmates reported how their plant was growing. They shared how they had saw the changes take place as they continued to water and make sure their plant receives good sunlight. And what you may asked happened to my plant? Absolutely nothing. My plant did not grow because I didn't go through the proper process with faith and patience.

Those that are under your care are a seed. We must cultivate and water them with the water of the WORD of God. We must give them sunlight (worship and praise and adoration showing them mercy, correcting and loving them with the right heart).

With faith and patience I encourage you to take this challenge.

May God bless you richly as you embark upon this joyful journey of speaking God's scriptural blessings over your child(ren).

# DAY 1

# YOUR CHILD'S ROOM

Father I ask for you to come into (YOUR CHILD'S NAME)'s room and release your Holy Spirit to saturate every square inch. I declare that this is a room where (YOUR CHILD'S NAME) can seek your face and worship you freely and unhindered.

I declare your conviction, creativity and problem solving anointing is in this room for (YOUR CHILD'S NAME) to walk according to your assignment over their life.

May you expose and identify anything that is hindering your presence from flowing fully into this room.

I declare that this room is a place of your SHALOM. You said in your word that you grant your beloved rest.

I declare (YOUR CHILD'S NAME) is your BELOVED and (YOUR CHILD'S NAME) is able to sleep with ease and refreshing day by day and night by night.

I declare that this room is a "no fly zone" and every foul thing that would try to move through the airwaves is bound up, ceases and desist right now in Jesus name.

Father today I loose your life, revelation and light into this room. I loose your purity into this room and I release the joy of the LORD into the atmosphere of this room.

Father thank you for your angels encamping around this room because I fear you.

You said that the fervent and effectual faith filled prayer of righteous person bears fruit and is answered by you.

> *"Confess your faults one to another, and pray one for another, that ye may be healed. The effectual fervent prayer of a righteous man availeth much."*
>
> **James 5:16 KJV**

Thank you for your presence is completely dominating this room and blessing (YOUR CHILD'S NAME) today In Jesus name.

# DAY 2

# REJOICING

*"You turned my wailing into dancing; you removed my sackcloth and clothed me with joy, 12 that my heart may sing your praises and not be silent. Lord my God, I will praise you forever."*

**-Psalm 30:11-12**

(_INSERT YOUR CHILD'S FIRST NAME_) I declare that you are rejoicing in your God because he has turned all your sadness into dancing! He has taken away your clothes of sadness and sorrow and given you clothes of joy!!! Today your heart is singing the praises of your OWNER and GOD. You cannot be silent today because of your God that is giving you the great joy of praising him forever!!

In Jesus name!

# DAY 3

# OBEDIENCE

*If you are willing and obedient, you shall eat the good of the land;*

**-Isaiah 1:19**

(_INSERT YOUR CHILD'S FIRST NAME_)You are walking today with a willing and obedient spirit to the Heavenly Father. Today you are eating the best of the land in situations that you are facing in your life. You will eat the best in how you relate to others, in the classroom, in your studies, in your resources.

In Jesus name!

# DAY 4

# FAVOR SHIELD

*Surely, Lord, you bless the righteous; you surround them with your favor as with a shield.*

**-Psalm 5:12**

(_INSERT YOUR CHILD'S FIRST NAME_)You are surrounded by a shield of favor, meaning you have great advantages in how people treat you today as you are walking in obedience to the Scriptural instructions of your Heavenly Father. The first thing people are running into today when in your presence is the shield of Favor that is placed around your life. Today you are expecting and anticipating the favor of God to surround you in all you do. In Jesus name.

# DAY 5

# THE SECRET PLACE

*Whoever dwells in the shelter of the Most High will rest in the shadow of the Almighty.*

**-Psalm 91**

(_INSERT YOUR CHILD'S FIRST NAME_)Today you are living from the Secret Place of the Father's presence. You are a good investor and making time to seek the Father's heart through prayer, study and constant thinking upon his words. You are delivered from all oppression and resistance of the evil one in all forms because of your staying in God's presence all day long. In Jesus name.

# DAY 6

# WISDOM INCREASE

*And Jesus kept increasing in wisdom and stature, and in favor with God and men.*

**-Luke 2:52**

(_INSERT YOUR CHILD'S FIRST NAME_)Today you are growing in wisdom, your physical body is prospering in health, wellness and top performance as you are treating your body well. Today you are mentally sharp and walking today with clarity of thought. Your speech is spoken with precision and seasoned with salt. Others are eating life from the words that you are speaking today. Today you are emotionally stable and walking with the Shalom of God within your emotions. This day your will is in alignment with the will of the Heavenly Father. You are walking out the will of God for your life this day. This is the day that people will treat you well because of your obedience to the Father. Today even when you experience conflict the Father will cause you prevail because of your attitude of humility, faith and of trust in him. In Jesus Name.

# DAY 7

# MEDITATION

*"This book of the law shall not depart from your mouth, but you shall meditate on it day and night, so that you may be careful to do according to all that is written in it; for then you will make your way prosperous, and then you will have success."*

**-Joshua 1:8**

(_INSERT YOUR CHILD'S FIRST NAME_)Today I declare that the book of Instructions the Bible is finding it's home in your mouth. Your mouth is speaking of the WORD of the LORD with confidence. You will grow in your desire to walk in obedience to all that is written in the SCRIPTURES for your success. Today as you are walking and believing the WORD, your Father is making your way prosperous today and you are having a GOOD SUCCESS! In Jesus name.

# DAY 8

# LIGHT FOR YOUR PATH

*"Your word is a lamp to my feet And a light to my path."*

**-Psalm 119:105**

(_INSERT YOUR CHILD'S FIRST NAME_)I declare today that the WORD of the LORD the Bible is a lamp to your feet. You are walking by the guided revealing light of the WORD of God and the WORD of the Kingdom is a light, bringing clarity, understanding and wisdom to every path and decision you are making today at home, at school and in your heart and mind. In Jesus name.

# DAY 9

# MAXIMIZING YOUR DAY

*This is the day which the Lord has made; Let us rejoice and be glad in it.*

**-Psalm 118:24**

(_INSERT YOUR CHILD'S FIRST NAME_)Today I declare is THE DAY and you are celebrating your Heavenly Father's creation of TODAY. You are walking with a heart of joy and rejoicing in the day.

You are prospering today as you rejoice in the day that the LORD has given you.

Today is your 86,400 seconds of rejoicing to go out and achieve all that the LORD has put in your heart for this particular day.

You are redeeming today, wisely investing in the right moments. Your priorities are according to the goals you have set for this day.

You are goal oriented and destiny driven.

Today you are GLAD in your day because as you are focusing on the right activities, your day will bring forth a profit of righteousness.

TODAY doors are opening, wrong relationships are moving out and fruitful relationships are being strengthened.

In Jesus name!

# DAY 10

# THIRST FOR GOD

*O God, You are my God; Early will I seek You; My soul thirsts for You; My flesh longs for You In a dry and thirsty land Where there is no water. 2 So I have looked for You in the sanctuary,*

*To see Your power and Your glory.*

**-Psalm 63:1-2**

(_INSERT YOUR CHILD'S FIRST NAME_)I declare that The Heavenly Father is your God.

I declare that early each day you will seek God with your whole heart while he may be found.

I declare that you are sensitive and recognizing your spiritual need for food.

Today you are being refreshed by the water of the REFRESHING WORD OF GOD! As you are studying the word TODAY you are being drawn into a Secret Place of worship and adoration.

Today by the grace of God, you are experiencing the power of God in your life and you are bringing him glory by doing exactly what you are created to do! In JESUS NAME.

# DAY 11

# KNOWING YOUR GOD

*"...but the people that do know their God shall be strong, and do exploits."*

**-Daniel 11:32**

(_INSERT YOUR CHILD'S FIRST NAME_)I declare that you are a child of the KING.

Today you are coming into a deeper knowing and intimacy with your Heavenly Father through study of scriptures as well as praise and worship. As a result of your time with your Father today you are stronger and you are going to do great exploits in all you are putting your hands to!

You are in common union and fellowship with the one True Living God. You are walking in the footsteps of King Jesus.

Today You are achieving, taking territory and dominating in your circle of influence in Jesus name.

# DAY 12

# SINGING AND PROCLAIMING

*Sing to the LORD, bless His name; Proclaim good tidings of His salvation from day to day.*

**-Psalm 96:2**

(_INSERT YOUR CHILD'S FIRST NAME_)Today I declare that you are singing to the LORD.

I say that you are blessing the name of the LORD!

I declare that you are speaking of his good news and all he has done in your life, how he has saved you from destruction and purposelessness into a life of meaning and fulfillment.

Today you are recounting all the great things he has done and will do as your Savior. In Jesus name.

# DAY 13

# CALLING TO THE LORD

*"Call to me and I will answer you, and will tell you great and hidden things that you have not known."*

**-Jeremiah 33:3**

(_INSERT YOUR CHILD'S FIRST NAME_)Today I declare that as you call out to your Father he is answering you today. Your Father is also showing and telling you great and hidden things that you have never known before.

He is showing you great things in all areas because he loves you and is concerned with seeing you succeed today. Today you are calling out to the LORD without shame, apprehension or embarrassment because TODAY you are growing in your trust your Heavenly Father. In Jesus Name.

# DAY 14

# FREED FROM INIQUITY

*"Establish my footsteps in Your word, And do not let any iniquity have dominion over me."*

**–Psalm 119:133**

(_INSERT YOUR CHILD'S FIRST NAME_)Today I declare that your footsteps are being established in the word of the LORD your Father and that no lawlessness, rebellion or iniquity is having dominion or rulership over your life.

Today You will not be tricked, deceived or convinced by wicked people to do stupid things that break your communication with your Heavenly Father.

Today I declare You are walking with a willing heart today and no only righteousness and peace is ruling over your heart today as you are studying the word of God with the heart to do obey. In Jesus name.

# DAY 15

# BLESSED IN PURITY

*"Blessed are the pure in heart, for they shall see God.*
**-Matthew 5:8**

(_INSERT YOUR CHILD'S FIRST NAME_)Today I declare you are empowered to prosper. You are blessed today and your heart is pure. Your heart is pure because it is open completely for your Father and today you are seeing God in a new way working in and through your life. You are joining the Father where he is at work today. In Jesus name.

# DAY 16

# SUCCEEDING THROUGH CHRIST

*I can do all things through CHRIST who strengthens me.*

**–Philippians 4:13**

(_INSERT YOUR CHILD'S FIRST NAME_)Today I declare you can do all things through the Anointed King of kings Jesus. Today I declare you ARE DOING ALL THINGS THROUGH CHRIST WHO IS STRENGTHENING YOU. Today Jesus is granting you strength through the Holy Spirit to accomplish great things. Today you are walking with the confidence that you CAN and will do ALL THINGS. In Jesus name

# DAY 17

# JOY IN HIS PRESENCE

*You will make known to me the path of life; In Your presence is fullness of joy; In Your right hand there are pleasures forever.*

**-Proverbs 16:11**

(_INSERT YOUR CHILD'S FIRST NAME_)Today I declare that your Heavenly Father is making known to you the path of LIFE.

Today I declare that you are living from being in the PRESENCE of the OWNER of THE EARTH and UNIVERSE.

Today you are finding fullness of JOY in the PRESENCE OF THE OWNER and your joy is full today!!!! In Jesus name.

# DAY 18

# COME AND GET REST

*"Come to Me, all who are weary and heavy-laden, and I will give you rest."*

**-Matthew 11:28**

(_INSERT YOUR CHILD'S FIRST NAME_)Today I declare that you are coming closer to the LORD in every situation.

Whenever you may feel weary today I declare you are going to the LORD JESUS and he is giving you rest today because of your trust and reliance on him.

In Jesus name!

# DAY 19

# THE LORD IS DELIVERING YOU

*And the Lord will deliver me from every evil work, and will preserve me for his heavenly Kingdom; to whom be the glory forever and ever. Amen.*

**-2 Timothy 4:18** (WEB)

(_INSERT YOUR CHILD'S FIRST NAME_)Today I declare that the LORD is delivering you from every evil work!

There is no weapon formed against you today that will prosper.

Today you are preserved for the KINGDOM of GOD.

Today you are giving glory to the HEAVENLY FATHER by completing the work he has given you to do today.

Your gift, talents and abilities are being activated today to bring God honor and praise. In Jesus name.

# DAY 20

# ACCEPTED BY YOUR FATHER

*For Yahweh won't reject his people, neither will he forsake his inheritance.*

**–Psalm 94:14** (WEB)

Today I declare that you are resting in the truth that the LORD won't reject you.

Today I declare your confidence that THE LORD won't forsake you because you are his INHERITANCE. You are The LORDS prized possession. Your Father values and treasures you and will not reject you because today you are one with a humble heart and a contrite spirit. Today you are nearer to your Father than you were yesterday because you are seeking the LORD while he may be found. In Jesus name.

# DAY 21

# DRAWN BY LOVE

*Yahweh appeared of old to me, saying, Yes, I have loved you with an everlasting love: therefore with loving kindness have I drawn you.*

**-Jeremiah 31:3** (WEB)

(_INSERT YOUR CHILD'S FIRST NAME_)Today I declare that the Father loves you with an everlasting love. Your Father proved his pure love for you many centuries ago through the sacrifice of his son Jesus on your behalf.

Your Father is drawing you today with his lovingkindness.

You are walking in full confidence and an awareness of the Fathers drawing upon your heart today.

In Jesus name!

# DAY 22

# YOUR NEEDS
# RE SUPPLIED

*My God will supply every need of yours according to his riches in glory in Christ Jesus.*

**-Philippians 4:19** (WEB)

(_INSERT YOUR CHILD'S FIRST NAME_)Today I declare that all you needs are supplied by your Heavenly Father.

You are living in a world of abundance. You are deeply aware that your Father's pathways drip with ABUNDANCE. You are not lacking in any area. You are fully supplied by the riches of the home headquarters from where your Father's throne is HEAVEN. In Heaven there is no lack, poverty or scarcity. Today you are wholeheartedly aware that your Heavenly Father is the owner of the EARTH and he is generous to give you everything you need today(Psalm 23 and Psalm 24).

In Jesus name!

# DAY 23

# HE KEEPS HIS
# COVENANT

*Know therefore that the LORD thy God, he is God, the faithful God, which keepeth covenant and mercy with them that love him and keep his commandments to a thousand generations;*

**-Deuteronomy 7:9**

(_INSERT YOUR CHILD'S FIRST NAME_)Today I declare that the LORD and HEAVENLY FATHER of the Universe is YOUR GOD. Your God is faithful to you today. Your God is keeping his sacred covenant agreement with you. _____ know that today God is showing you mercy because you LOVE him and are keeping his commandments. He is blessing you and all that is in you to a thousand generations. In Jesus name.

# DAY 24

# YOU ARE TAUGHT OF THE LORD

*And all thy children shall be taught of the LORD; and great shall be the peace of thy children.*

**-Isaiah 54:13**

(_INSERT YOUR CHILD'S FIRST NAME_) I declare today that you are taught from the LORD in all your studies, in your relationships, in your health, in your money, in any areas that you lack clarity in, the LORD is giving you clear teaching through his WORD the BIBLE TODAY.

Your peace is great in all you are doing today. You are being led by the Peace SHALOM of God. Today, If there is no peace, you will not continue in the direction where you lack God's peace. In Jesus name.

# DAY 25

# SURROUNDED
# BY ANGELS

*"The army of the Angels of Lord Jehovah surrounds his worshipers and delivers them."*

**-Psalm 34:7**

(_INSERT YOUR CHILD'S FIRST NAME_)Today I want to declare and remind you that the LORD's angels surround you this day.

Understand with all confidence and confess that you are covered and surrounded by the LORD'S mighty angels. You are a true worshipper, as you are worshiping the LORD you are being delivered from danger by his angels. So today I declare a spirit of worship upon you. In Jesus Name.

# DAY 26

# YOU ARE AN EXAMPLE

*"You are the light of the world. A city set on a hill cannot be hidden;*

**-Matt 5:14**

(_INSERT YOUR CHILD'S FIRST NAME_)you are the light of the world. You are the revelation or the example of what God wants to do in every area of society. People are watching you today because God's light of his holiness is flowing out of your life. I declare your faith in the LORD Jesus makes you stand out like a city that's at the top of a hill.

You aren't fitting into circles of mediocrity because you were made to stand out as a leader and example in how you are serving and walking out a life that honors Jesus. You are the light of the world! In Jesus name.

# DAY 27

# SALT OF THE EARTH

*"You are the salt of the earth; but if the salt has become tasteless, how can it be made salty again? It is no longer good for anything, except to be thrown out and trampled underfoot by men.*

**-Matt 5:13**

(_INSERT YOUR CHILD'S FIRST NAME_)You are the salt of the Earth.

You are God's seasoning in the planet. All of creation is looking at you and knowing that your Heavenly Father is with you. Just like salt you are walking today bringing flavor through your unique personality and bright smile.

You are God's flavor in the Earth. _____ You are God's preservative and when he is looking upon your city and granting mercy it is because you are there walking in obedience to his instructions.

Today you are God's purifier just like salt, all the creation sees how you are walking and your life provokes others to purify their lives. In Jesus name.

# DAY 28

# HIS SPIRIT IS UPON YOU

*The Spirit of the Sovereign LORD is upon me, for the LORD has anointed me to bring good news to the poor. He has sent me to comfort the brokenhearted and to proclaim that captives will be released and prisoners will be freed.*

**-Isaiah 61:1**

(_INSERT YOUR CHILD'S FIRST NAME_)The Spirit of the Sovereign Lord is resting upon your life. Today You are endorsed and equipped from Heaven to achieve. Today it is your God given right to succeed at the work you put your hands to. You are walking in heavenly wisdom in all areas today.

You are able to know the finer differences between good and evil, good and best, good and God. In Jesus name.

# DAY 29

# PROSPER EVEN AS YOUR SOUL PROSPERS

*"Beloved, I pray that in all respects you may prosper and be in good health, just as your soul prospers."*

**-3 John 1:2**

(_INSERT YOUR CHILD'S FIRST NAME_)You are prospering successfully in your mind. Your mind is orderly: you are capturing every unproductive and useless thought, kicking the bad thought out in Jesus name and replacing the bad thought with God's royal thoughts over your life!

You are walking today with creative solutions to problems. I declare clarity of thought over your life today!

You have the willpower today to say yes to The Fathers goals and plan over your life.

I declare You are guarding your morning today and instead of wasting willpower on checking foolish things online, you are investing willpower in saying yes to the little things in the Bible that is waiting for you today to release blessing in your life.

Your emotions today are under your control.

I declare you are a master over your emotions. You are not following how you feel today. Instead you are choosing to do what is right and are you are moving forward in Fathers goals for your life. I declare you will be quick to forgive and slow to get angry. I declare you are quick to listen and slow to speak. I declare that you are speaking out soft answers and turning away wrath of foolish, rebellious, contentious and argumentative conversations. I release today that you are a peacemaker and are BLESSED by your Father. In Jesus name.

# DAY 30

# THE LORD IS YOUR LEADER

*The Lord is my shepherd I shall not want...*

**-Psalm 23:1**

(_INSERT YOUR CHILD'S FIRST NAME_) Today I declare that the LORD is your OWNER and your SHEPHERD meaning your LEADER.

Today you are led by the LORD into great situations.

You are led in your thoughts, you are led in your words, you are led in your emotions and you are led in your joy by the LORD. You are rejoicing in the fact that today you are led and protected by the LORD he is giving you protection, provision and promoting you to amazing opportunities of blessing and abundance as you walk with him. In Jesus name.